All the words written in this book are 100% Chad Williams. Quotes from famous people are attributed.

Mathieu René, Créaturiste made the fox puppet on the cover and Mystery Max (the detective puppet you'll see often) with a costume by Sarah Lafferty. Additional building credits are on the last page in this book.

Initial design templates by Eviory Studios (licensed). Some vector images (modified) from public domain.

All photos were taken by Chad Williams and Z. Briggs with the following exceptions: Richard Termine (p. 84), RJ Lewis (p. 79), Martin Timm Photography, Inc. (p. 29), Jennie Neufeld (p. 68), Angelito Jusay (p. 76), and Lauren Khalfayan (p. 85).

50 Hand Puppet Techniques
Hidden Secrets & Tricks Revealed
by Chad Williams

FOREWORD

I first met Chad Williams in 2007 while in rehearsals for Drama of Works' production of Warhol. I was one of the four humans in the show who brought to life not only a beautiful puppet of Andy Warhol by David Michael Friend but a collection of various Campbell's soup cans and other found objects. Chad and his partner, Z Briggs, were making their first of many documentaries about the Puppeteers of America conference "Puppet Rampage" in St. Paul, MN. While I had been in the NYC puppet scene for a few years, I was still relatively wet around the ears. I remember being in awe of Chad and Z, how they knew so many puppet people from all over the country. But that is one of the beautiful things about the puppetry community, it is a great big family of people who take their playing seriously. We are in it because it brings us immense joy and the ability to communicate in ways that we cannot otherwise express through other mediums.

My first true love was puppetry. I grew up in the era of Jim Henson and my entire being was deeply shaped by his many masterpieces. But I fell head over heels in love with puppeteering when I was nineteen doing a summer abroad in Paris studying with master puppeteer Alain Recoing at the Theatre Aux Mains Nues. The translation is "Theater of the Naked Hand", and for many hours every day for over a month with burning aching arms, I learned the art and craft of hand puppetry. These days I am no longer puppeteering due to ALS, but my great love of the art form still beats in my chest.

Reading this book was such an immense delight for me. It was deeper than a trip down memory lane because puppeteering is a physical visceral experience, the memories of my training are in my very bones. Because we as puppeteers are simultaneously sending out our own life force while also surrendering to the will of the puppet we are breathing life into, the connection for me is also soulful.

My hands, which have been still in my lap for many years now, kept remembering or rather feeling that same electricity with each practice Chad mentions. This is a wonderful collection of the foundational bones upon which all hand puppets are based. A training in the grammar of movement and ideology, much like the positions and barre work are at the core of ballet. Unlike any ballet class I ever took, there is humor woven in between the theory, history, and exercises, which is also at the root of puppetry. Chad encourages the reader to play while also instilling the need for clarity and focus, which can be a difficult line to walk for anyone who has been left to their own devices. He also finds a way to incorporate the more esoteric aspects of puppetry, which is why it remains a true love of mine. Puppetry began as ritual for and the sacred and profane. Ritualized storytelling through puppetry brings us out of the way of our mental chatter and busy senselessness of the everyday. It brings us into the present moment. Experiencing the breathing of a puppet can actually help us remember to breathe deeper and connect more with what is truly important in life. We hold this power in our hands and this book is a key to access it.

Lindsay Abromaitis-Smith

(she/her) is a witch, artist, herbalist, writer, and pleasure activist.

Hand Puppetry
Two-Finger Style

This book is a technical manual for how to perform the Two-Finger Style of hand puppetry, also known as the Modern Method or Double Finger: ダブルフィンガー (Japanese) or 双指 (Mandarin). If you are a beginner puppeteer, it will also teach you how to create the illusion of life.

Hand puppetry, also known as glove puppetry in some parts of the world, is a very special performance art that is ever-evolving. It can elicit laughs as the characters look like tiny humans, but wielded properly can also shock or horrify. In truth the greatest practitioners of this style have every move choreographed, every bit of baked-in symbolism understood, can interact safely with an audience and can communicate their message clearly without resorting to muddy movements or gimmicks.

For centuries, puppeteers in Europe and America used either one finger or two in their hand puppets' heads with a "whatever is more comfortable for you" attitude. Just as in the world of magicians, puppeteers kept the inner workings of their craft a secret and many times performers had to reinvent something that already existed previously. There was no tradition of passing on information to anyone outside of family or trusted troupe members. This all changed in the early 20th century with Paul McPharlin's famous book that cataloged all the puppeteers in America, uniting them. Puppeteers came together to form organizations, share techniques and collaborate. With puppets now appearing on television, the world became a lot smaller.

Many of the American practitioners of hand puppetry in the 1900s who were widely considered to be "the best" were self-taught and used one finger in the puppet's head. That changed in the 1970s when the innovative and highly respected Paul Vincent Davis embraced Two-Finger Style, raising the skill ceiling for the form. His hand puppetry could be extremely technical with beautiful and controlled movements. He influenced many puppeteers to change from One-Finger to Two-Finger, including Mary Churchill whom he would go on to marry. Paul and Mary performed for decades at Mary's Puppet Showplace Theater in Brookline, Massachusetts (which is still open today).

Award-winning puppeteer Carol Fijan saw Paul perform at a festival and invited him to collaborate. Together with acclaimed puppeteer Larry Engler they created the highly influential book **Making Puppets Come Alive** which championed Two-Finger. Carol and Paul taught Bart Roccoberton this style and he has passed on this knowledge to generations of students at the Puppet Arts program at the University of Connecticut. Z. Briggs learned from Bart, she taught me and I am passing the torch on to you.

CHAPTERS

My method of teaching this style
is 5-fold, the five fingers that together
grasp hand puppetry's base elements.

As these over-the-top titles suggest, you should
always have fun while you perform puppets. Do take
learning and perfecting techniques seriously, but
remember that having fun will help you find new
ways to perform and help you have a good
time. Play is a fundamental pillar of
good puppetry!

STRETCH FIRST DON'T HURT YOURSELF OMG

Before You BEGIN

Puppetry is an inherently physical performing art. You must remain comfortable while performing, otherwise you risk injuring yourself. Older puppeteers have switched hand puppet styles from 1 finger to 2 in order to ward off arthritis or support weakening joints.

Before you begin each performance and before you explore the contents of this book, you should stretch your fingers, wrists and shoulders. Employ a full-body stretching routine like Yoga or Tai Chi and get serious about preserving your flexibility while strengthening your body.

If just one part of your body fails, you will not be able to perform.

Stretch your FINGERS

1
Shake out Hands
Get the blood flowing to the tips of your fingers

2
Play Piano
Quickly stretch each finger up and down

3
Diamond #1
Push your index fingers and thumbs together

4
Heart + Triangle
Bring your index fingers down, middle fingers up, repeat for each finger set

Maintain each stretch for 10 seconds.
If it hurts, stop right away.

Opposite Direction

Push each finger set down
one at a time while keeping
the others together

Neutral Stretch

Pull index and middle
fingers up together, pull
down with others together

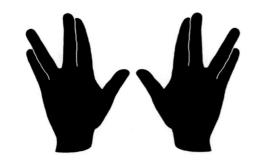

Arms Up

From Neutral, stretch
thumb out and stretch
ring + pinky out

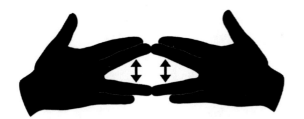

Diamond #2

From Arms Up, both hands
touch middles and rings,
push to form a diamond

"More Stretching, Less Stressing"
– some motivational poster

9

Fingers Apart
Stretch fingers as far apart from each other as possible

10

Clench Fists
Gently close your hand into a fist, clench but not with tension

11

Palms Together
Push hands together, elbows to wrists should form a horizontal line

12

Fingertips
Slowly pull hands apart starting at palms, keep fingertips together

Back of Wrists

Push the back of your wrists
together, arms form a
horizontal line

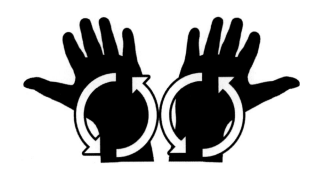

Helicopter

Rotate your wrists in big
circles, one way 5 times,
opposite way 5 times

Shake Out Hands

Shake your hands out
again. Your fingers should
feel loose and limber.

Your fingers should feel loose yet strong.
You are now ready to perform!

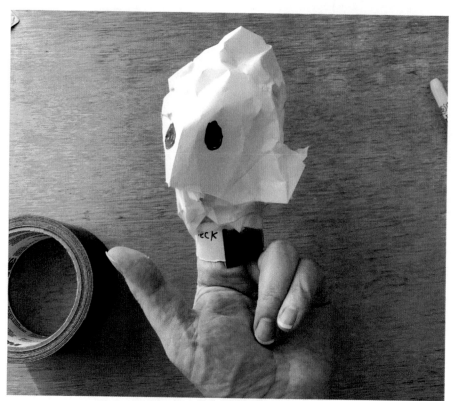

Creating Quick Puppets

Keeping your fingers free while having a simple puppet head is the ideal way to learn. Create a Quick Puppet before you begin.

Materials Needed

Toilet paper roll   2 Sheets of plain white paper   Scissors   Strong tape

Masking tape or similar   Black marker

01

Cut and Tape the Roll

First, take your scissors and cut the toilet paper roll vertically (hotdog style). Place your index and middle finger inside the roll, and gently curl it around these fingers with your other hand. When the roll is comfortable yet snug on your fingers, tape it in place with the strong tape.

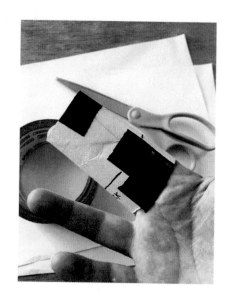

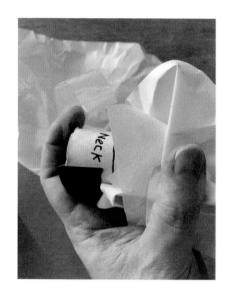

Crumple the Paper

Mark a line with the marker 1" from the bottom edge of the roll. Crumple two sheets of white paper and arrange them onto the toilet paper roll. Form a head shape. Tape it in place and tape it all to the roll. Make sure you keep exactly 1" of neck at the bottom.

Draw Two Eyes

Finally, draw two big eyes onto the paper head with your marker. It is important to know where your puppet is looking at all times, so make sure the eyes are large. That's it! You are now ready to begin.

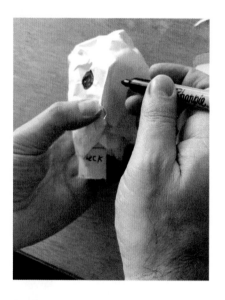

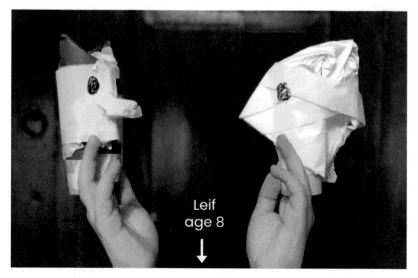

Leif
age 8

Now Play!

Play with your new puppets. Have fun!

1

The Water of Life

This chapter will detail the most basic skills for any puppeteer. These skills can be used for any style, be it hand puppets, marionettes, object puppetry, rod puppets, mask, etc.

A puppet is
any inanimate object *skillfully manipulated* to create the illusion of life.

That is the most basic universally agreed-upon definition in the United States of America (perhaps the world too). One cannot bring a puppet to life without touch. When you touch a puppet with the intent to bring it to life, your spirit flows from your head down through your arm, coursing up your hand and into the object.

Your spirit becomes like water. The puppet is a vessel you must pour yourself into. Water adopts the shape of its receptacle - your spirit will fill any object(s) you physically connect with through touch.

"...Be formless, shapeless, like water. If you put water into a cup, it becomes the cup. You put water into a bottle and it becomes the bottle. You put it in a teapot, it becomes the teapot. Now, water can flow or it can crash.

Be water, my friend." - Bruce Lee

What is a Dead Puppet?

When you sever your connection with the object, it cannot move or breathe or think and it ceases to hold the possibility for life. We call that a "dead puppet". While it may be convenient for a puppeteer to leave a puppet on stage for a moment to manipulate another object or move an item or scenery, you should never do this. It creates confusion for the audience and breaks the illusion. It becomes harder to hold the audience's focus as they are now asking themselves why the puppet is now lifeless. The character you skillfully brought to life is now sitting in full view of the audience with a blank expression or sitting in an uncharacteristic way. Your spirit has left it behind, and everyone knows it.

It is possible for your puppet to become "dead" even when you are physically touching it. In all puppet forms, you must look at the puppet you are manipulating 100% of the time in order to maintain the illusion of life. If you look away to reach for a prop or become distracted, your consciousness leaves the puppet momentarily and it may begin to slouch or act unnaturally until you look back at it properly. If you must look away from your puppet for some reason, have it not look directly at the audience and busy itself with a motion that does not necessarily require good posture, like looking around, thinking, or walking. **This will prevent "death".**

Puppet is "alive"
Good posture

Puppet is "dead"
Bad posture

Posture

If your puppet has a human-like figure, it must have a posture to match. Make sure your puppet's spine is straight and not slouching - unless you have decided that a slouch is part of its unique character. Hand puppets look best when they are standing straight up.

When you operate a hand puppet, hold it directly in front of you - not in front of your chest but in front of whichever shoulder is attached to the arm you are using. Your arm should feel comfortable and not tense. The puppet's head is about at eye-level with your eyes.

Remember that we are looking for **"the illusion" of life, not "an imitation" of life**. All the movements that you perform will be exaggerated pantomime. It should feel over-the-top, a heightened reality that borders on the surreal or fantastic. Even when using hand puppets to portray a realistic scene, you will need to use bigger than usual movements. Remember that in theater, actors use different body language in order to easily communicate their intentions to the people sitting in the back row of the audience.

NOW:

PUT

YOUR

PUPPET

ON
YOUR
HAND

YAY!

breath

Take a deep breath.

Notice how your chest puffs out when you inhale,

your spine straightens and your head moves up slightly.

Now exhale. We will be doing an exaggerated version of these

movements in miniature, using your hand. With your bare hand, stick

your index and middle fingers up toward the sky, holding your thumb and ring /

pinky together. Your two fingers have become the neck and head, your palm has

become the chest. Below the meaty muscles at the bottom of your hand is the

puppet's waist.

Now, put a puppet on your hand. Breathe deeply and at the same time, make the same breathing motion with your puppet. Try different breaths, short gasps, long sighs. Always breathe along with your puppet. Feel the connection between your body and this miniature version of yourself. Some puppeteers call this "the breath of life". You have breathed life into something that before contained no life.

Now, take off the puppet, put it down and step away. Look at the puppet. With no physical connection to you, it cannot move or breathe - it is truly dead. In this way, according to master puppeteer Sandy Spieler, **you have just re-enacted your own birth, life, and death.**

Breathe in and
tilt whole body up,

Breathe out and
tilt whole body down

focus

Take a look around.

That was some pretty heavy stuff!

Don't worry, as long as you are alive, your puppet still contains the potential for life. Now, put the puppet back on your hand. Find the puppet's eyes. Make sure they are pointing in the same direction, or if it has no eyes / multiple eyes, decide which direction its head must face in order to see. Which way is its nose pointing?

Look around with your puppet. Look up, look down, look all around. Look behind them. Your puppet is curious, looking way down at your feet, looking far up at a spiderweb on the ceiling. Always know where your puppet's eyes are looking - you should be able to draw an invisible line from its eyeballs to whatever it is looking at. We call this focus.

Try looking and breathing at the same time. You can do it!

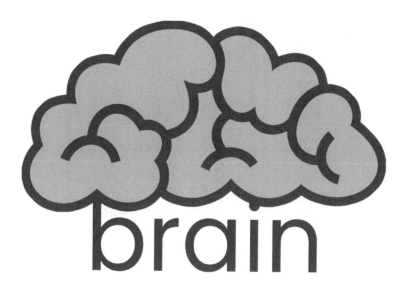

brain

Stop.
Think.
Decide.

Before any action, your puppet must show that it took a moment to decide what to do. Before it takes a step, it must decide which direction to move, and so on. This greatly enhances the illusion of life.

Hold the fingers in your non-puppet hand up like blades of grass. Now, bring up your puppet facing the audience (away from you). Look around, and eventually see the grass. Instead of immediately crossing to it, have the puppet STOP for a moment. What is your puppet thinking? "What is that? Have I seen that before? Maybe I could go get that."

Once you have decided on an inner monologue and thought about it for a moment, now the puppet is ready to make a decision. It faces the audience and silently thinks, "I will go over there." Now it turns toward the grass, walks over to investigate. What happens next is up to you.

Taking time to think is one of the three most important tools available to you. If your puppet does not show a capacity to STOP, think, decide, then move, your illusion will be weak. Even in a scene where there is great urgency, the puppet must have a brain. Also, the puppet doesn't have to tap its head every time you want to communicate "I AM THINKING". Just pause all movement and **let the moment breathe.**

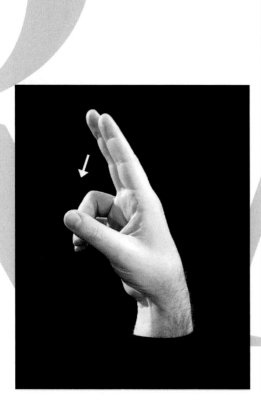

Tilt head down,
tap one arm on
the puppet's chin

see, think, react

Did you get all that? It will come in time with practice. So far your puppet can breathe, see with its eyes, and think about what to do next. Now let's put it all together.

Bring up the grass again (your non-puppet hand with its fingers up). Let's pretend that the grass is completely unexpected, something the puppet has never seen. Repeat the same scene from before - the puppet enters, looks around, notices the grass. This time give it a big reaction. "What is that!? Wow! I have never seen that before! Is it safe?" Give the puppet a reaction to what it is seeing, and think about how we can communicate its feelings, what it is thinking, to the audience. What are some different emotions it can have to react to this new thing?

This time, when it crosses to investigate, let its feelings lead its inner monologue and its movements. "Ugh, I hate that! I can't stand it! Disgusting!" or "Are those bones? Oh no, I can't do this, I'm too scared!" or whatever you can think of. Try starting the scene with different emotional takes and end it differently each time. Remember to draw an invisible line between the puppet's eyes and what it is looking at, remember to breathe, **remember to take your time** and have the puppet think about what to do next.

See.

Think.

React!

SECRET #1 TECHNIQUE

Finger Twist

Looking around the stage with your puppet, its entire body moves to accommodate the head. However, due to the special nature of the Two-Finger Style, we can do a more subtle movement.

How to do the Finger Twist

1 Inside your puppet's neck are two fingers. While maintaining pressure on the inner neck with both fingers, twist the fingers around each other.

2 Your puppet's head will turn with a beautiful subtle movement. Now twist the other way - your puppet will turn its head while its body remains stationary.

3 If you have trouble with this technique, it may be that the puppet's neck is too tight against your fingers or so open and wide that you cannot easily turn the head. If this is the case, add a little foam or cut the neck open to resize it.

Twist fingers left and
right, body should not
move (just head)

02

A Rock-*Solid* Foundation

This chapter is about understanding the fundamentals of a specific puppet form: hand puppetry.

photos by Martin Timm Photography, Inc.

To be more precise, as there are many different ways on how to perform a puppet on your hand, this book teaches the **Two-Finger Style** of performing a hand puppet.

"I hated every minute of training, but I said, 'Don't quit. Suffer now and live the rest of your life as a champion.'"

Muhammad Ali

Muhammad Ali was a professional boxer and activist, known as the greatest heavyweight boxer of all time and the most celebrated sports figure of the 20th century.

The Three Styles
A History

Chinese, European, Modern. These three styles are siblings - separated by time and space but all related by the human hand.

HOW MANY FINGERS?

01

European Style
1 Finger in the head
Thumb and Middle form arms
Ring and Pinky unused

02

The Modern Method
2 Fingers in the head
Thumb forms one arm
Ring and Pinky form other arm

03

Chinese Style 布袋戏
3 Fingers in one arm
Index finger in head
Thumb forms one arm

There are many combinations of where you can stick your fingers inside a hand puppet. Some American puppeteers like Great Arizona Puppet Theater's Nancy Smith tuck their middle + ring fingers into the puppet's chest (unused), while traditional Catalonian puppeteers put their index, middle and ring fingers in the head.

It is impossible to know yourself unless you first understand others. I highly encourage you to watch the performances of puppet companies from other countries to see how they do things differently. It is often humbling to see the level of technical skill attained by puppeteers the world over.

布袋戏

Bu Dai Xi

Hand puppetry can be traced back to its ancient Eastern Chinese origins as Bu Dai Xi (pr. *boo-die-she*) - an action-packed, miniature version of the Beijing operas of the day performed on the street. Inside the puppet, three fingers form one thick arm and only one finger is inside the neck / head. A skilled puppeteer can flip their hand around inside the puppet, perform an intricate dance or conduct a lightning-fast fight scene.

" They are designed to mimic human movements accurately with an absolute minimum of technical interface. "

- Chinese Theater Works' master puppeteer Stephen Kaplin

Some Bu Dai Xi shows may include intricate weapon fights, puppets flying through the air or changing their expressions. As Bu Dai Xi spread throughout Asia, a similar form began to take shape in the West.

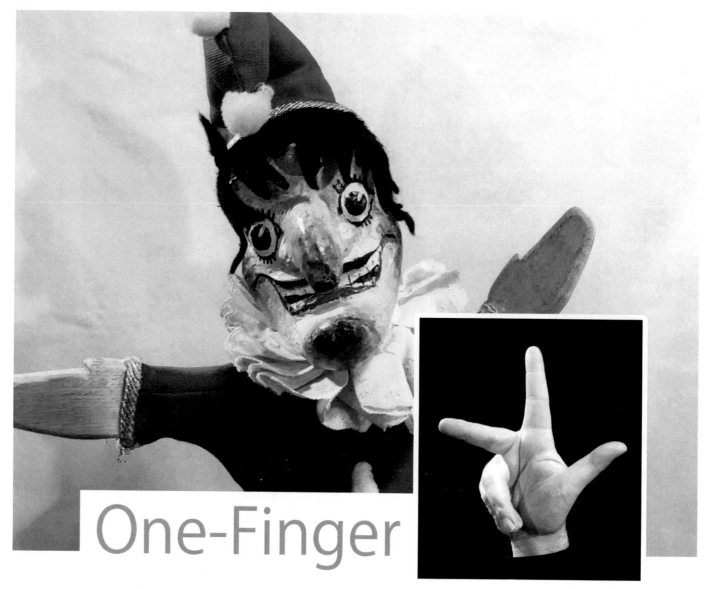

One-Finger

Pulcinella and his European kin

Raunchy, political street theater that entertained and spat fire at the societal ills of the day erupted on the streets of 1600s Italy. The puppet Pulcinella and his European descendants Polichinelle, Kasperle, and Mister Punch (pictured above) popularized a new style where a roughly manipulated puppet conversed directly with the audience. This egomaniacal character who does whatever they want evolved from archetypes in the Italian improvised theater tradition of Commedia dell'arte. Inside these puppets three fingers formed both arms and the neck/head. The remaining two fingers tucked underneath and were hidden by oversized costumes.

Two-Finger

The Modern Method

Two-Finger Style, popularized in 20th century America by Carol Fijan, Paul Vincent Davis and others, allows a puppeteer more strength in the hand puppet's head and neck and arms. This strength allows for more nuanced movements than Pulcinella, and more balance between limbs than Bu Dai Xi. There are no extra fingers to hide in the costume. In addition, there are two hidden techniques that can happen inside the puppet's body to create superbly subtle movement. It is not as technical or high-flying as its Bu Dai Xi counterpart, making it easier for beginners. One does not need special flexibility training to properly maintain finger posture but it remains an innately physical performing art. It's as 'middle of the road' as you can get.

Major Stances
MINOR STANCES

All finger movements must be performed from a **stance**, a pose that your fingers must form in order to begin a specific movement. There are two major stances that most moves spring from, and three minor stances for less common movements.

Each stance can be done with just one puppet arm, or both. From Neutral, either puppet arm can transition into these stances while the other stays firm.

MEDIEVAL FESTIVAL NYC 2011 PUPPET SHOW

Glove puppets ...
they can't do what
a person can do.
You have to figure
out how to *cheat.*

Paul Vincent Davis

Neutral

NEUTRAL

Fingers at Rest

First is Neutral Stance, where your fingers are crossed in front of the puppet's body. When your puppet is not moving, not talking, not walking, always return to this stance. It is the beginning of all movements and where every action chain eventually ends. From this stance you can transition into any of the other stances or apply a move. Your fingers should be at rest when in Neutral.

It does not matter which puppet arm is in front of the other. Either is fine.

If a puppet ends a speaking line and poses in anything but Neutral, it will seem unnatural (unless this is part of your pantomime). In this case, try to find a moment to quickly shift into Neutral that will not disrupt the scene or draw attention.

Draw Back

DRAW BACK

Get Ready

The second stance is Draw Back. From Neutral, draw your ring and pinky fingers back toward the puppet's body and bring your thumb to the puppet's side. Your hand becomes flat. From Draw Back, most moves can be performed. It is the most common beginning stance for all moves.

Each stance can be done with just one puppet arm, or both.

Minor *Stances*

While most moves can be performed from Draw Back, there are certain movements that will naturally start elsewhere. These are less common but will strengthen your performance by adding variety and range.

Try creating each stance with your hands. Remember that these poses can be done with a single puppet arm in certain situations.

ARMS UP

Surprise!

From Neutral or Draw Back, stretch your ring and pinky fingers and your thumb back and away from the middle of the puppet as far as they will allow. Your hand forms a flat W shape. This is the natural next step of Draw Back.

ARMS BACK

Extra Surprise

Pull both arms back behind the puppet's back while moving the head forward / down.

ARMS FORWARD

Point, Pray or Plotting

From Draw Back, stick both arms forward. They can stay separate or come together.

03 *Fiery* Fingers

This chapter explains how to move your fingers to perform different moves. Moves are specific motions that help the audience to understand what the puppet is thinking and feeling, and supports the illusion that the puppet is alive. Each move begins from a stance, continues into a recognizable middle, and then either returns to a stance or goes on into the next movement in an action chain.

Chaining moves together is a good way to draw the audience's focus as one puppet speaks or emotes, but each gesture must not blur into the next. If you commit to a specific movement, you must remember to do the beginning, middle, and end of that motion. Give each move the time it needs to be extremely clear.

"The spirit of fire is fierce, whether the fire be small or big; and so it is with ~~battles~~ Puppet Shows."

Miyamoto Musashi, probably

Musashi is the most famous samurai to ever live, winning 61 duels and dying only to old age. His book on sword technique and philosophy, The Book of Five Rings, inspired this book!

Moves

Most of the non-specific gestures you will
see in a hand puppet show fall under three
categories: **Poke, Chop and Sweep**.
They can be performed in any direction, but
the overall movement must be the same.

Poke

 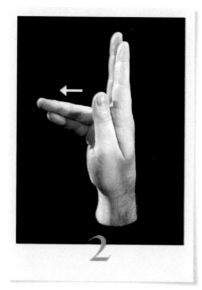 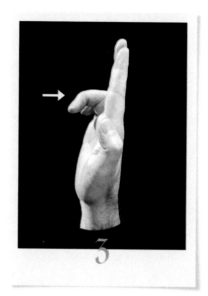

POKE

A Quick Point

A Poke starts from the Draw Back Stance. The puppet's arm (either one) extends straight out in a direction until it cannot go any further, then retreats back from whence it came. This is generally used to point, indicate, or punch.

Let's break the Poke down into its most mechanical form. To produce this most basic gesture you must move your fingers not once but four different times. Start at Neutral Stance, move to Draw Back stance, then Poke out with a puppet arm, then back to Draw Back, finally back to Neutral.

Can you hold the Poke out for a while, or end by chaining to another move? Yes. Yes you can.

Chop

CHOP

Quarter-Circle Indicator

The Chop is similar in its utility to point or emphasize a line, to indicate or to attack. Instead of the puppet's arm extending straight out, it starts by facing in a direction (usually up) and follows a circular motion to its desired end point, then reversing to go exacty back to where it began. The Chop should always be a quarter circle.

This can be used in any direction from any stance, with either arm.

Sweep

SWEEP

360 Degree Circle

The Sweep can be used to indicate a vague notion or to address multiple things at once. It is a 360 degree circular motion that starts from any stance, any direction. With one arm, make a full circle in the air. Always return to the exact position as before.

Using your thumb to do a Sweep can be done easily without moving the rest of the puppet's body. Using Ring / Pinky to make a Sweep will require the whole puppet's body moving in tandem.

It is very hard to do a full circle with both arms at once, so just use one at a time. However, with both arms starting together, you can use them to each draw half of a full circle.

Uncommon *Moves*

When not gesturing or pointing, hand puppets have a wide array of moves at their fingertips (pun intended). There are far more that exist than what are described here, you should always seek to discover more interesting ways of moving in every performance.

WAVE

Starting with your Ring / Pinky arm up, quickly move it down and back up.

CLAP

Start at Arms Up Stance, quickly bring both arms together then apart.

COME HERE

Extend one arm forward, then Chop up or towards the puppet's chest.

SLEEP
Lay puppet on playboard, back facing audience, eyes hidden, breathe.

FLEX
Start at Arms Up Stance, bring arms down into Draw Back Stance, and back.

COVER FACE
Tilt the body down and cover either the ears, eyes, mouth, or nose.

BIG REACTION
Start at Neutral Stance, then quickly back up while moving to Draw Back.

"In puppetry, the whole body of the puppet is involved, his movements exaggerated. *He is literally wrenched by emotion.*"

Paul Vincent Davis

Conveying emotion without speaking is one of the main goals of puppet theater. A puppet can literally speak **"I am happy"** but it can also convey this by looking slightly up and bouncing around a little bit, by having an excited energy to their movements, by clapping and moving faster. Visual language is always the more powerful way to connect to the audience, as puppetry is an innately visual medium.

The following moves are universally recognized as specific emotions by audiences around the world. There are more to discover and some cannot be easily described here, such as shyness or disgust.

Happy! Tilt the puppet's head up 15 degrees (slight). Bounce around, clap, dance, embue every movement with fun. Give a big "yay!" with Arms Up Stance.

Sad. Tilt the puppet's head down 15 degrees (slight). Cry, sigh, make slower movements. Shake head "no". Breath is everything to conveying sadness.

Surprise! Jump backwards (away from the surprising thing) into Arms Up Stance. A classic bit is to have your puppet turned away, have the surprise tap their shoulder. Slowly they turn until they see it - then boom!

Fear. From Draw Back Stance or having the puppet hold the sides of its head, shake your hand with vigorous vibration (not too much). Use this bit sparingly as it gets old quick.

Anger. Bring the puppet's arms up and slam them down into Arms Forward Stance. Every movement is faster than before, every word accentuated with a move that stops just as quick.. Tense your whole hand.

Movement
Foundations

JAB, STRONG, FIERCE

This also applies to emotions, walks, breathing, and so forth.

Just as each move has a beginning, middle and end, they can be performed with three levels of intensity - Jab, Strong, or Fierce. Jab is a weak or gentle motion, quickly done and only the puppet's arm moves. Strong moves the body slightly with its decisive and slower movement. Fierce is a huge exaggerated movement where the puppet's entire body participates - the biggest, grandest motion possible.

 GO BACK TO MOVE FORWARD

A general rule for any movement is to always move backward before you move forward. That applies to walks, arm movements, breaths, and others. It can be as simple as a quick, short, almost unseen motion back before going ahead with a move. If you are doing a Fierce move, the initial backward movement should mirror the intensity of what's to come. The more emphasis you put on moving backward first, the more the audience will feel the significance of the motion.

To emphasize a move even further, just STOP.

Stop all movement, action, everything - stay frozen and let the moment breathe. This will help the audience process what they have just seen.

Characters on stage need not necessarily be frozen in time, they could be watching, breathing, doing everything but moving. A good rule for using STOP is to figure out if a scene is pure movement and dialog. If there are no breaks in the action, if characters are either speaking or moving without any pause, that is a good indicator to find some places to STOP. This is different than a character pausing to think before they act.

> ## "American puppetry is too muddy."

Muddy is what we call a string of unrelated actions with no clarity. If you begin an action chain, you must understand how each move supports what is being communicated to the audience. How does each move look from the audience's perspective? A single clear movement is far superior to a series of loose, wiggly motions. Children move a puppet without thinking - professionals communicate with clarity.

Some puppeteers cover up their lack of skill with fast movements. A poorly defined move executed at high speed can seem exciting to the audience. This philosophy of "speed over quality" has been used in gimmicky puppet shows but should not be viewed as something to strive for. Instead, a good rule is that slow movements can be more beautiful. **In a puppet show the rules of gravity and time do not necessarily apply.** To emphasize a movement and make it more interesting, more beautiful or more intricate, slow down time and take however long you need to complete it. Finally, use this sparingly or else your audience will get bored.

Find Your
CHOREOGRAPHY

How to discover dynamic movements that makes sense

1. To create solid choreography for your puppet plays, imagine yourself (your whole body) in the puppet's place. In your rehearsal space, act out the scene using exaggerated pantomime movements. Instead of reciting the script, say out loud what the character is thinking and feeling during each moment. Keep a running inner monologue going.

2. Now try it out with puppets. Their capability is different, so translate what you were doing in each moment into their limited moveset. Keep saying the character's inner monolog out loud.

3. Then do the scene again but completely silent, carefully noting the major emotions, movements and locations of your character. Make sure everything makes sense without dialog - you are still just acting out movements to the inner monolog.

4. Once it makes sense without words, add the real script back in. Now you are performing the new choreography atop the scripted words. In this way, you can create excellent movements that feel natural and expertly conveyed your character's thoughts and emotions.

4

Walking
with
Wind

In this chapter, you will learn various techniques from around the world that will strengthen your performing style. You will learn to walk, to move your wrist and arm in conjunction with your fingers. Wind can also mean tradition - old traditions and new ones. It is difficult to know oneself unless you know others.

Martha
Graham
said:

"Movement never lies. *It is a barometer* telling the state of the soul's weather to all who can read it.

Martha Graham was an American dancer and choreographer known as "The Mother of Modern Dance".

How to Walk

To walk with your puppet, to move it freely around stage, means that you too must move. Your feet, which are normally firmly planted while the puppets are standing still, must be ready to gently walk around. Remember that a hand puppet must maintain proper posture at all times including during a walk or run. That means your whole body will need to lean, sway, and move.

Stand up. Form a Neutral Stance with your dominant hand. Move your entire arm, from your elbow to your fingertips, up and down, over and over. You must not exceed 2-3 inches going up or down, but also moving too little (under 1 inch) is poor. This is the basis for all walks. Now, while moving your arm up and down, walk the puppet 3 feet (1 meter) to the left, then to the right - all while maintaining good posture. Make sure to move your own body to allow your arm the freedom to move without straining.

Finally, while the puppet is walking, twist your wrist slightly with each step. This will cause the puppet's body to twist and better mimic human movement. In the first step, twist its body to the left, ending the twist when the puppet's "foot" lands. For the next step, twist its body to the right, and so on. When you walk with your own body, your left foot moves forward at the same time your right arm and right shoulder move forward. In the next step, it alternates: your right foot moves forward as your left shoulder and hand do. This is the action we are mimicking in miniature.

Just as every move has a beginning, middle and end, your walk must terminate somewhere. Decide where your puppet will stop and make it a definitive end. A sloppy ending will ruin the illusion that this character can walk and actually has legs. Remember that below the playboard you must imagine your puppet to have imaginary feet that can trip or kick. As all moves are exaggerated pantomime, so too must your walk end with a determined final step.

Exercise: walk a puppet around the stage and STOP, then turn to look at something. Walk to that something, keeping the puppet's eyes focused on it at all times. Turn around and repeat. Practice this by using a playboard or do it in front of a mirror.

Stopping

SECRET TECHNIQUE #2
Turn-Around Twist

If your puppet is on your right hand and you walk to stage left, you will eventually hit a wall. You can go no further left, and if you attempt to turn back to the right, your wrist will be unable to fully do so. You might be able to turn the puppet's head and body slightly, but it will cause you great pain to try and force a full turn without moving your own body to the puppet's left side. In this uncomfortable position you will be unable to perform as well as when the puppet is comfortably in front of you, facing the way your wrist naturally wants to move.

AAARGH!

The solution is a technique called **Turn-Around Twist**. With your right hand facing stage left, twist the puppet to face you and continue this twist until it faces stage right. It must be a quick 180 degree upstage twist in one fluid motion. Try the same with your left hand facing stage right. Twist the puppet to face you and then continue this twist until it faces stage left. Practice walking your puppet from left to right, turning around using this technique and walking in the opposite direction. Walking this way will feel unnatural at first.

Twist wrist upstage, puppet now faces the opposite direction

The *Five* Walks

One thing we can absolutely borrow from Bu Dai Shi is how their puppets walk. These puppets walk in the same way that Chinese actors playing archetypal characters in Beijing opera have walked for hundreds of years. Each of the four major roles has their own set movement, and it can instantly give the audience a lot of information about the character. Inspired, we will use these ideas to create five main walks for Two-Finger Style.

Basic Walk

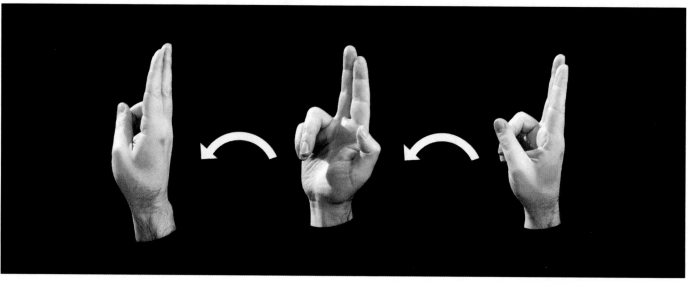

Above: 2 steps

BASIC

Generic, Standard Walk

The Basic Walk is perfectly average. The puppet moves up and down within 3 inches while moving left or right on stage. While they move, twist their body slightly to the left or to the right with each step. End the walk with a definitive last step.

Utilize your puppet's arms as you walk. I usually keep the arms mid-way between Neutral and Draw Back (*see middle photo*).

inspired by: Sheng 生

In Bu Dai Xi, Sheng is the main male role. Like the other major roles, there are several subtypes (Laosheng - old man, Wu Sheng - warrior, etc). They are respectable people: scholars, nobles, heads of households.

Feminine Walk

Above: 2 steps

FEMININE

Hip-Swinging, Grace

Start with a basic walk. Now, your wrist becomes the puppet's hips, and you should sway the hips to the left and right with every step. Adding to this, twist its body more than usual as you walk. Imagine your hand is a paintbrush pointed down at a piece of paper that lies flat at the bottom of your wrist. If done correctly, the paintbrush should paint a perfect Figure 8 with every two steps. Slow down time to make it easier on yourself - the puppet isn't going anywhere fast. If you cannot do the Figure 8, just focus on swinging the hips to indicate femininity.

inspired by: Qingyi 青衣

Qingyi (also known as Zheng Dan 正旦) is the most important role in every opera. Qingyi (*pr. king-yee*) is usually a wife or mother, a full-figured feminine woman who is virtuous.

Old Person Walk

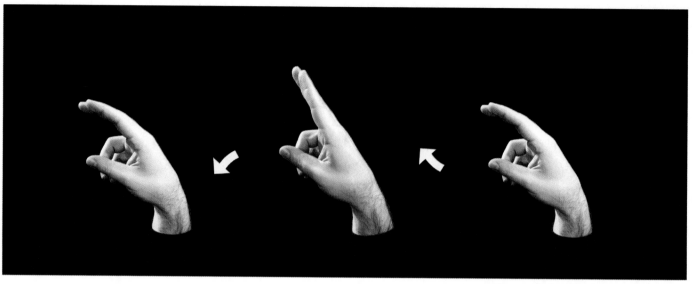

Above: 1 single step

OLD PERSON

Slow, Curved Posture

Curl the puppet's spine down towards the ground until they are looking at the floor. Its back should not be parallel to the ground but be curved. Now, every step begins with the puppet's head moving up as its hips move forward. As its body steps forward, its head comes back down to the beginning pose. This motion resembles the movement of an inchworm or caterpillar.

This movement should be subtle and slow. Imagine a person old and withered, every step they take is a great effort.

inspired by: Lao Dan 老旦

Lao Dan (*pr. lahw dahn*) is the old woman, a clever person whose costume is subdued in color and design. Her voice is natural and not high-pitched.

Warrior Walk

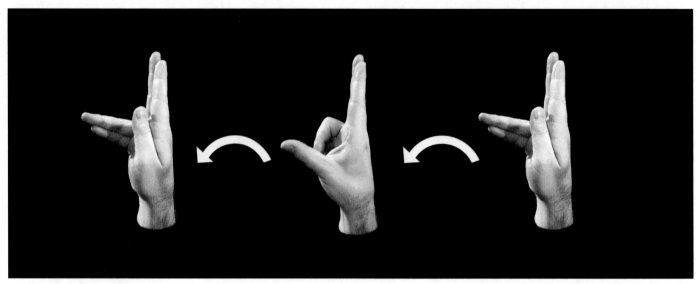

Above: 2 steps

WARRIOR

Confident, Heavy, Military

Warrior Walk is like Standard Walk, but with every movement isolated and with a strong feeling. Every turn, every step with Warrior must be extremely crisp. Think of military precision, how a trained soldier moves. Instead of merely twisting their body with every step, the Warrior also extends their fists into the air in front of them. You can also have them say "Hah!" with certain moves to emphasize their strength and battle-readiness.

Imagine this character wearing heavy boots that stomp with each step.

inspired by: **Jing** 净

Jing is a male role with a painted face, a very forceful character with exaggerated movements. Jing is rough and mighty, strong and sometimes bull-headed. He moves with a confident swagger.

Clown Walk

Above: 2 steps

CLOWN

Light, Graceful, Fun

The Clown Walk is two-fold. With every step, your puppet must tilt to the side 15 degrees while reaching out one arm in that same direction - almost like a one-armed Arms Up Stance. The unused arm tucks in to the chest. Then into the next step, tilt to the other side while extending the other arm, tucking in the unused arm to the chest. Remember to use light yet graceful steps.

When you walk with Clown, you must embody a fun spirit! Even when they turn to face the audience, it must be with a silly flourish. It's okay to smile and have fun with every move.

inspired by: **Chou 丑**

Chou (*pr. choh*) is the clown of Beijing opera, recognizable by a large circle of white makeup on their face. They perform incredible feats of acrobatics while always lighthearted and fun, foolish and likable.

Oh yes there are
Other *Walks*

There are many other ways to move your puppet around on stage. A ghost character can float, a magician can teleport from place to place, a baby can crawl. Try many different ways of moving around and think of a character or moment that would serve that walk best. Try to have as much variety of movement in your show as possible.

Once you are comfortable walking your puppet on stage, moving around and looking around, try to incorporate everything you have learned thus far. Remember that your puppet can breathe, can STOP, can gesture and utilize different moves to communicate. Face the audience and prepare yourself to begin talking.

Remember that just like moves, walks can be performed to three different intensities: **Jab, Strong, and Fierce**. How pronounced your puppet character walks tells the audience a lot of information about them. Are they a Fierce Old Woman, or a Strong Clown, a Feminine Warrior etc.? Mix and match different characteristics and use these roles as a starting point for your original characters.

Jab

Quick, light or softer walks with more subtle movement.

Strong

Standard walks with average weight, speed, and movement.

Fierce

Big, heavy walks that take their time. Make each step intense with lots of tension.

Run!

Same but faster

Once you can perform each walk with ease, try doing the same thing but twice as fast. **Maintain the specific movements that make each walk recognizable.** This is a run. Now try the walks at half speed. You can achieve more beautiful and purposeful movement when you slow down time.

photo by Jennie Neufeld

Enter and Exit

Human actors on a stage are in character the moment they first set foot in the wings - as soon as the audience can see even a small part of them, they are expected to walk, act and behave as their characters. Puppets do not just appear on stage - they walk, run or slide there. They can teleport in or jump, they can fall in or ride an unseen elevator, but every entrance or exit must be a choice. The puppet must begin moving in character before the audience can see it (below the playboard). **Remember: no dead puppets.**

Lessons from
MISTER PUNCH

The Punch & Judy tradition from England is world famous. Punch, who evolved over centuries from Pulcinella in Italy, has dangly legs in front of his bottom sleeve. This gives him the ability to sit with his legs splayed out on the playboard. When a puppet has an extra appendage, a gimmick or special effect, the audience expects to see it in action. However, you should only use this type of thing <u>once</u>. Every time the puppet does something extraordinary, the next time they repeat it half of its power will be gone. The same is true for jokes. Every time you use the same joke or gag on stage, its power is halved.

Let's apply that to walks. The first time you have a really dynamic chase scene in your show, it will be a really special and fun moment. If you do the same type of chase scene again, or if you have puppets move in a similar manner again, both it and the previous incarnation will seem less special. If you choose to have a specific movement that draws attention, remember that you should find a different way or variation instead of repeating the same thing again. **Mister Punch only sits and crosses his legs once.**

6 Things All Children Think Are Funny

Sneezing, Farting, Snoring, Burping,

Chasing, and "When Things Go Wrong".

Oh, and comedy comes in threes.

Shouting into the
VOID

In this chapter you will learn how to speak through a puppet. You will learn what pitfalls to avoid, and there are many. You will learn the basics of split focus and how to successfully operate two puppets at once. Finally, puppeteers love to "talk shop" and go on at length about their craft - *some even write whole books about it* - but I will keep the philosophy section at the end very brief.

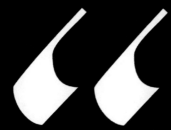

We speak with more than our mouths. *We listen with more* than our ears.

Fred Rogers, puppeteer

Known as "Mister Rogers", Fred was the creator, showrunner, puppeteer and host of the preschool television series "Mister Rogers' Neighborhood", which ran from 1968 to 2001.

How to Speak

Stand up and speak a sentence out loud as if you are on stage. An actor will use their entire body to emphasize visually what they are thinking or feeling, and so should a hand puppet. Did you thrust your head and neck all around when you spoke? No. So: **do NOT wobble a hand puppet's head when it speaks.** It can gesture, move, walk, any kind of movement but do not wiggle its head. This will break the illusion and it just looks plain bad.

Face the Audience

When a puppet speaks, it faces the audience. It moves and gestures! This is called drawing focus. If there is another character on stage at the same time, it must face the puppet that is speaking and it must not move. This is called giving focus. Most hand puppets do not have moving mouths. It is imperative then that the puppet who is speaking be the only thing moving on stage, and when it is done speaking it should stop moving completely. This helps the audience understand who is talking.

There are exceptions to this rule: the puppet speaking a line may briefly face away from the audience to gesture or add emphasis. However, when two puppets are on stage it becomes very important to stick to this rule.

How to Ask A Question:

If you are going to interact with the audience directly, there are certain paths for success. Never ask a question for which you are not prepared for the answer. If you ask the audience if they prefer the Knight to win the battle or the Dragon to win the battle, you had better be prepared for either eventuality. Also, when given the chance to speak during the show, the audience is unpredictable. What time of day it is, whether or not the audience has eaten lately, what's going on in the audience's life, all of these are factors that will influence what they say for good or for bad. We can iron out all of these potential problems with some quick solutions.

1	Never ask an open-ended question. Instead ask questions that can be answered in 1 word.
2	Use a 'fill in the blank' sentence with an obvious answer instead of asking a question.
3	Prepare a strong in-character reason for not doing what the audience wanted.
4	If you give the audience a true choice between two things, have those things ready to incorporate into the show.
5	Be prepared for no answer at all. If the audience is silent, find a way to move on without it.
6	Never nag or beg for the audience to participate. Some audience members don't feel like talking and that's okay.

If the audience is fixated on something, **acknowledge it only once** and move on quickly. This will let them feel heard and allow you to carry on with the show.

Hostile Audience

Above all else you must maintain control of the audience. You are in charge and must do your utmost best to maintain a safe atmosphere for the show to exist. At any point if things get out of hand, if the audience begins to stand up, yell out inappropriately, throw things, threaten or otherwise act poorly, it is your responsibility to stop the show and calm things. Allowing a hostile audience to grow into an angry mob can have dire consequences. Knowing this, you must do your absolute best to never stop a performance as it both obliterates the illusion of life for the remainder of the show and it may empower a hostile audience to get just as bad again.

Never heckle the audience, single someone out or make someone feel bad for how they responded or acted. Always make yourself the victim of the joke. Make the audience feel good about themselves and they will behave better. Kindness will always triumph over anger.

Training
The Audience

Whether or not the audience will behave or be endeared to your show depends on what you do before the performance even begins. If you are in a theater, the audience already understands what is expected of them and only the stage is illuminated. If you are in a non-traditional setting, you must do your best to control the lighting, ambient sound and other aspects to ensure the audience can easily focus. During the preshow, give the audience some general rules about expected behavior and what will happen on stage. If they are given a task, dance move, repeated line or anything to do later during the performance, show them exactly how to do it yourself first and then practice it all together immediately afterward.

You can ask for the audience's help at any time with specific language. Do a countdown from 3 to give everyone time to focus first. Repeat the same type of introduction to a question, action or movement so they know what is coming. If the response is muddied, gently and firmly tell them to try it again on your mark.

When you have trained the audience and they respond correctly during the show, it makes them feel good.

photo by Angelito Jusay

Two at *Once*

To perform two hand puppets at the same time, simply put one puppet on each hand and walk them onto stage. What is their relationship to each other, to the audience? How can a puppeteer divide their spirit between two puppets, or make sure both puppets maintain good posture and not become "dead"?

The answer is **split focus**. Instead of looking directly at your puppet, or even the puppet that is currently speaking and gesturing, set your sights directly between both puppets. Stare out at the audience, pick a point in space and look at that while keeping both puppets in your eyes' periphery. You will be able to see both puppets at once and ensure their movements stay crisp. By practicing a two-puppet scene over and over, you will become accustomed to what needs to happen physically and will be able to relax and focus on acting through both characters.

EXERCISE:

Put on two puppets and hold them in front of you. Have one face the audience while the other faces the first puppet. Have the puppets count to 10, alternating who is speaking. Whomever speaks a number must face the audience while the other looks at the speaker. Go back and forth until you reach 10. Do this again with different character voices, different emotions, get the feeling of "the speaker faces the audience, the listener faces the speaker". Mechanical movement will become fluid movement.

Always look in between two puppets, keep them in your peripheral vision.

The advantage of one puppeteer performing two puppets at the same time is that your hands can perfectly mirror each other's movements. Two different puppeteers may be able to perform a single character each more beautifully but will not be able to match each other's movements like a single puppeteer can. However, this should be used sparingly.

When you are walking two characters at once, alternate both who is moving up and who is moving down while (if possible) simultaneously alternate who is tilting left or right. This will help the audience believe that they are two completely separate entities, and not just the same person twice.

Mirror Mode

What makes puppetry *special?*

When an actor presents themselves to the audience, all eyes are on them. They strive for truth, but in reality they are simply pretending to be someone else. A puppeteer is an actor too, but one who can command the focus of the audience - presenting a neutral third party (the puppet) that has been built for this particular role and nothing else. The audience understands that at the end of the show, an actor will remove their makeup and go home as a regular person. However, a puppet cannot take off its paint, or its costume, it is only alive when a puppeteer brings it to life - for one scene or one particular moment in time. A skilled puppeteer who can fool the audience with the illusion of life is assisted by the audience's innate subconscious knowledge that this moving object is NOT in fact alive. It is not pretending to be something else - it merely IS.

Builder
or Performer?

Does a performer also need to be a good builder? Does a builder also need to be a good performer? In either case, no, but it helps to have some working knowledge of both. Very few puppeteers are excellent at every single aspect of puppetry, and many choose to focus on a single aspect of it. An exquisite performer should understand how to quickly repair their puppet, and the greatest builder should understand the challenges of performing on stage. Whether you choose to be in front of the curtain or behind it, you should always practice kindness. Kindness to the audience, to the people involved in your production, and kindness to yourself.

Why Puppets?

I ask this question to myself before I begin any work on a new puppet production. Could this be accomplished with regular actors on a stage? If the answer is "Yes", then I do not continue, the idea dies right then and there. If the answer is "No", the only way this could be presented on a stage is with puppets, then we begin our work of creating a new story. Puppets can grow or shrink physically, you can set fire to them, they can break apart into tiny pieces and be put back together again - there are no rules when it comes to puppet theater. Therefore the only theater productions you should create that are "puppets only" should be the ones where having puppets makes it work.

"Daddy,

Are the puppets *real?*

After a show, some puppeteers are quick to show that it's all just a trick, that puppets aren't real - all to satisfy an audience's curiosity or to help sew interest so a child may grow up to become a puppeteer and continue the art form. Some puppeteers insist that a puppet is real, they are alive and that "they are only sleeping" when not on stage. Which is true? Are they both correct?

Puppets carry with them the lineage of sacred objects. The first puppets were symbolic figures used by ancient humans to represent gods and forces of nature. Priests who used masks or shadow figures in religious rituals were the first true puppeteers. Consider also that the human brain is hard-wired to recognize faces. The reason that the illusion of life works is because in the back of our minds we want these characters to be real. Some people see faces in everyday objects, it's the same thing. Puppetry has existed in many different forms throughout human history. So, are the puppets you manipulate real?

The great puppet master Bernd Ogrodnik once told Z. and me:

"Of course they're real! I am real, and they're me!"

I believe this is the correct answer to the age-old question. The puppet is a vessel waiting for a spirit to inhabit it. When you're in there, it's real.

It's *you.*

photo by Lauren Khalfayan

That's All, Folks!

Thank you for reading this book!

I am a firm believer that **" the rising tide raises all boats "**. When the entire puppetry community is more technically skilled, it will benefit us all. Potential puppeteers looking for training have often told me that there is scant information about how to do what we do on the internet. This is the reason I have written this manual and offer free guides on how to build and perform hand puppets online. If you have any questions, contact me at **WonderSparkPuppets.com**

Dedications

This book is dedicated to my two sons Leif and Finn. If you ever wanted to be a puppeteer like your Dad, here is a guide!

This book is also dedicated to the memory of Jim Rose, a kind and wise puppeteer who taught me much about puppetry.

Finally, I wouldn't be here without the love of my life and puppetry mentor, Z.! Thanks for asking me to be in your slam piece all those years ago.

about
Chad Williams

Chad Williams has been performing hand puppets for family audiences in New York City and beyond since 2009 as WonderSpark Puppets. As Co-Artistic Director, he wrote, directed and performed over 15 puppet plays that played in theaters, parks, libraries and private spaces hundreds of times each year. Chad performed his original works in Taiwan and Thailand, and has streamed live shows online since 2020. He has also worked as a teaching artist, helping kids create and perform their own original puppet plays in public schools. Chad is a Fulbright Specialist, Eagle Scout and UNIMA-USA board member.

Puppet Builders

Mathieu René, Créaturiste made the fox puppet on the cover of this book and Mystery Max (the detective puppet I used throughout). You can also see his work on pages 6, 29, 34, 58 (top right), 67, 79, and 87.

Lindsey 'Z.' Briggs made the puppets on pages 2, 13, 15, 35, 36, 58 (bottom left), 68, 76, 80, 82 and 84. Jim Rose made the Mister Punch puppet on pages 33 / 70.

Sarah Lafferty made the costumes for Mystery Max and puppets on pages 58 (top right), 79 and 87.

Special Thanks

Amy Rush and Justine Piontek proofread this book and gave amazing notes! Thank you both so much for making My (text) 'more' understandablable.

Thank you to my wonderful mentor Hua Hua Zhang for opening my eyes to a whole new world of technique and movement.

Thank you to puppeteer and clown Honey Goodenough who taught me what kids think is funny.

Thank you to Liz Joyce, Jim "Nappy" Napolitano, Roxy Myhrum, Allelu Kurten, and all the other puppeteers that helped us grow early on. To those kind enough to tell me when I made a mistake, I am forever indebted to you.

Finally, an extra special thank you to Lindsay Abromaitis-Smith who wrote the foreword to this book. As a puppeteer and dancer, every original work that she created was awe-inspiring and magical. I will always be a huge fan and consider myself super lucky that she said "yes!" to blessing this book with her inspirational words of wisdom. Discover her work at alchemyofthesole.com

Made in the USA
Las Vegas, NV
20 December 2023

83300826R00057